J 599.49
599.49
BRI

MORTON PUBLIC LIBRARY DISTRICT

A13001 707670

☑ **W9-BZX-813**

DISCARD

J 599.49 BRI
Britton, Tamara L.
Dog-faced bats

AR 3.8   .5 pts

DISCAR

BATS SET I

SEP   2010

MORTON PUBLIC LIBRARY DISTRICT
315 W. PERSHING
MORTON, ILLINOIS 61550

DOG-FACED BATS

Tamara L. Britton

ABDO Publishing Company

visit us at
www.abdopublishing.com

Published by ABDO Publishing Company, 8000 West 78th Street, Edina, Minnesota 55439. Copyright © 2011 by Abdo Consulting Group, Inc. International copyrights reserved in all countries. No part of this book may be reproduced in any form without written permission from the publisher. The Checkerboard Library™ is a trademark and logo of ABDO Publishing Company.

Printed in the United States of America, North Mankato, Minnesota.
042010
092010

 PRINTED ON RECYCLED PAPER

Cover Photo: © Merlin D. Tuttle, Bat Conservation International, www.batcon.org
Interior Photos: Alamy pp. 9, 11; Animals Animals pp. 5, 21; AP Images p. 19;
    Getty Images p. 13; © Merlin D. Tuttle, Bat Conservation International,
    www.batcon.org pp. 15, 17

Editor: Megan M. Gunderson
Art Direction & Cover Design: Neil Klinepier

Library of Congress Cataloging-in-Publication Data

Britton, Tamara L., 1963-
  Dog-faced bats / Tamara L. Britton.
      p. cm. -- (Bats)
  Includes index.
  ISBN 978-1-61613-390-0
  1. Cynopterus--Juvenile literature. I. Title.
  QL737.C575B75 2011
  599.4'9--dc22
                                2010006678

CONTENTS

DOG-FACED BATS 4

WHERE THEY'RE FOUND 6

WHERE THEY LIVE 8

SIZES 10

SHAPES 12

SENSES 14

DEFENSE 16

FOOD 18

BABIES 20

GLOSSARY 22

WEB SITES 23

INDEX 24

Dog-Faced Bats

There are more than 1,100 species of bats in the world. Dog-faced bats are members of the family **Pteropodidae**. Six species in this family are dog-faced bats. They are also known as **Old World** fruit bats.

One-quarter of all mammals are bats. Like all mammals, mother bats produce milk to feed their babies. But bats can do something no other mammal can do. They can fly!

Some people are afraid of bats. But these flying mammals are very helpful. Every year, they eat millions of insect pests. Bats help **pollinate** plants. They also plant trees by scattering fruit seeds as they fly. These helpful creatures are an important part of Earth's ecosystem.

Dog-faced bats are also called short-nosed fruit bats.

Where They're Found

Bats are found all over the world. The only places they do not live are Antarctica, the polar regions, and a few ocean islands. Bats are especially abundant in areas with a **tropical** climate.

The dog-faced bats dwell in tropical climates. They live in southern and southeastern Asia. They range from Sri Lanka to Indonesia and the Philippines.

The tropical climate allows dog-faced bats to hunt all year long. So, they do not **hibernate** like bats that live in **temperate** climates. But they do **migrate** to find ripening fruit.

Where They Live

Dog-faced bats have such a wide range that they live in many different **habitats**. They can live in forests or open country. Some live down at **sea level**. Others live at altitudes of more than 5,900 feet (1,800 m)!

Within their habitats, dog-faced bats live in a variety of homes. They live in caves, in deserted mines, and under the **eaves** of houses. Sometimes, the bats **roost** in hollow trees.

Some dog-faced bats actually build a home. They bite off the center seed string in a fruit cluster of the kitul palm. This leaves a hollow area in the middle of the cluster. There, the bats roost.

Dog-faced bats also **roost** in the folded leaves of talipot palms. They bite a palm leaf's ribs where they attach to the main stem. This causes the leaf's sides to droop along the stem, making a tent.

The dog-faced bat is the only Old World fruit bat known to build its own shelter!

Colonies of 6 to 12 bats live in these leaf tents.

A bat's feet each have five toes with sharp, curved claws. To roost, a bat grabs a roosting site with its feet and relaxes. The weight of the hanging bat tightens a **tendon** in each foot. This causes its claws to grip onto the roosting site.

SIZES

There are many sizes of bats. Some species of flying fox bats can be 16 inches (40 cm) long. They weigh 2 pounds (1 kg). Their **wingspan** is more than 5 feet (1.5 m)!

Other bats are very tiny. Kitti's hog-nosed bat is only 1 inch (2.5 cm) long. That is about the size of a bumblebee! These little bats weigh just 0.07 ounces (2 g). They have a 6-inch (15-cm) wingspan.

Dog-faced bats are medium-sized bats. Together, the head and body measure 3 to 5 inches (7 to 13 cm) long. The tail adds another 0.2 to 0.6 inches (0.5 to 1.5 cm). Dog-faced bats have a wingspan of 14 to 18 inches (36 to 46 cm). They weigh 1 to 4 ounces (28 to 100 g).

Like all bats, dog-faced bats are a member of the order Chiroptera. This Greek word means "hand wing." Bats have hands that are also wings!

SHAPES

Dog-faced bats have furry bodies. The fur is thick and silky. It is dark-colored shades of brown. Bats do not like their fur to be dirty. They spend hours combing and grooming their fur and cleaning their wings.

As its nickname suggests, a dog-faced bat's face looks like a dog's face. Dog-faced bats have large heads with large eyes and ears. Their pointed snouts have nostrils shaped like small tubes.

Dog-faced bats have two arms. Each arm has a hand with four fingers and a thumb. Each thumb has a claw.

A dog-faced bat's wing **membranes** stretch between its fingers and its body. The wing membranes also connect the tail and the legs,

forming a tail pouch. These black, elastic
membranes form short, wide wings. Short wings
are useful for flying among trees and bushes.

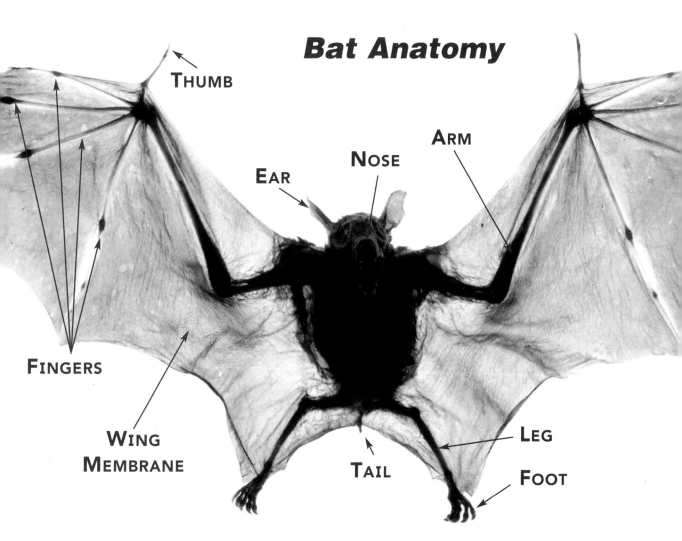

Bat Anatomy

THUMB

ARM

NOSE

EAR

FINGERS

WING
MEMBRANE

LEG

TAIL

FOOT

SENSES

Have you ever heard the phrase "blind as a bat"? Many people believe bats are blind. Yet bats can see! They can also hear, smell, taste, and feel.

Most bats are **nocturnal**. To "see" in the dark, about half of all bats use an additional sense. It is called echolocation.

To echolocate, bats make high-pitched sounds. These sounds come from their throats or noses. The sound waves go out and hit objects such as trees, buildings, or insects.

The bats catch the returning echoes in their ears. The echoes tell the bats where and how big the objects are. Bats use echolocation to fly safely and to find food. They also use it to avoid danger, such as predators.

Though dog-faced bats are **nocturnal**, they do not echolocate. Yet they can still find food, **roosting** sites, and other bats. They use their keen senses of sight, hearing, and smell instead.

Though they can see very well, dog-faced bats are color-blind!

DEFENSE

Dog-faced bats must defend themselves against many predators. Cats, dogs, and raccoons will eat bats. Owls, hawks, falcons, and snakes are also a threat. Spiders eat bats that get caught in their webs. And, some bats eat other bats!

Flying away is one defense against predators. Being **nocturnal** is another. Since bats fly at night, they avoid predators that hunt by day. Dog-faced bats also **roost** in safe, dark places during the day. Their dark color makes it hard for predators to see them.

The main threat to the dog-faced bat's survival is people. Fruit bats can damage or ruin fruit trees. And, large numbers of bats roosting in a tree

16

can actually kill it. So, farmers sometimes kill the bats to protect their trees. Other times, people cut down forests for timber and farming. That leaves fewer **habitats** and food sources for the bats.

Dog-faced bats eat pollen from the durian flower. Durian flowers open only at night. So, nocturnal bats are vital to spreading their pollen.

FOOD

Unlike most bats, dog-faced bats do not eat insects. They prefer the juices of palm dates, figs, guavas, plantains, mangoes, and chinaberries. Some species also eat leaves and flowers.

Bats are color-blind. So, they rely on their sense of smell to find good food. Dog-faced bats like fruit that smells sour or musty. They can travel 60 to 70 miles (97 to 113 km) to find food. When they find some, they may eat the food there. Or, they may take it with them to eat elsewhere.

As they carry the fruit away, dog-faced bats spread fruit seeds. After they eat, they eliminate more seeds when they pass waste from their bodies. From these seeds, bushes and trees will grow. In this way, bats help replant forests.

Almost 300 plant species depend on Old World fruit bats to spread their seeds and pollen.

BABIES

Dog-faced bats usually mate once a year. Yet some may breed twice a year. Mother bats give birth to one baby each time.

When giving birth, the mother bat hangs right side up by her thumbs. She catches her newborn in her tail pouch. The baby then climbs up and hangs on its mother's chest. There, it begins to nurse.

Baby bats are called pups. Newborn pups are large. They often weigh 25 percent of their mother's weight.

The pup drinks milk from its mother for about 45 days. At first, the mother bat must take her baby along when she goes to find food. Later, the baby can stay behind in the **roost**. When the mother returns, she easily locates her baby. Each pup has a special smell and squeak sound.

Female bats are mature when they are 5 to 6 months old. Male bats mature later, when they are 15 to 20 months old. When mature, dog-faced bats leave the **roost** to go out and find mates of their own. Soon, they have their own pups and take their place in Earth's ecosystem.

The dog-faced bat and its habitat must be protected. Products such as bananas and vanilla are available because the bats pollinate these plants!

GLOSSARY

eaves - the part of a building's roof that overhangs the walls.

habitat - a place where a living thing is naturally found.

hibernate - to spend a period of time, such as the winter, in deep sleep.

membrane - a thin, easily bent layer of animal tissue.

migrate - to move from one place to another, often to find food.

nocturnal - active at night.

Old World - all the continents of the eastern half of Earth, except Australia.

pollinate - when birds, insects, or winds transfer pollen from one flower or plant to another.

Pteropodidae (tehr-uh-PAHD-uh-dee) - the scientific name for a family of fruit bats.

roost - to perch or settle down to rest. A roost is a place, such as a cave or a tree, where animals rest.

sea level - the level of the ocean's surface. Land elevations and sea depths are measured from sea level.

temperate - having neither very hot nor very cold weather.

tendon - a band of tough fibers that joins a muscle to another body part, such as a bone.

tropical - having a climate in which there is no frost and plants can grow all year long.

wingspan - the distance from one wing tip to the other when the wings are spread.

WEB SITES

To learn more about dog-faced bats, visit ABDO Publishing Company on the World Wide Web at **www.abdopublishing.com**. Web sites about dog-faced bats are featured on our Book Links page. These links are routinely monitored and updated to provide the most current information available.

INDEX

A
arms 12
Asia 6

B
body 10, 12, 14, 18, 20

C
claws 9, 12
colonies 9
color 12, 13, 16

D
defense 14, 16

E
ears 12, 14
echolocation 14, 15
eyes 12

F
face 12
feet 9
fingers 12
flying 4, 13, 14, 16, 18
flying fox bat 10
food 4, 6, 14, 15, 17, 18, 20
fur 12

H
habitat 6, 8, 9, 13, 16, 17, 18
hands 12
head 10, 12
hunting 6, 14, 15, 18, 20

K
Kitti's hog-nosed bat 10

L
leaf tent 9
legs 12

M
migration 6, 18

N
nocturnal 14, 15, 16
nose 14
nostrils 12

P
pest control 4
pollination 4
predators 14, 16, 17
Pteropodidae (family) 4
pups 4, 20, 21

R
reforestation 4, 18
reproduction 20, 21
roost 8, 9, 15, 16, 20, 21

S
senses 14, 15, 18, 20, 21
size 10, 12, 13, 20
snout 12

T
tail 10, 12
tail pouch 13, 20
thumbs 12, 20
toes 9

W
wings 10, 12, 13